The Minotaur's Daughter

EVA LUKA

The Minotaur's Daughter

Selected Poems

Translated by James Sutherland-Smith

LONDON NEW YORK CALCUTTA

Slovenské
literárne
centrum

This book was published with the financial support of the
SLOLIA Board, The Slovak Literary Centre.

Some of these translations have appeared in *PN Review* (UK)
and *Tupelo Magazine* (USA).

The translator wishes to thank the Slovak Literary Centre and
Lita Fond for a stipendium in order to complete this selection.

Seagull Books, 2025

First published in English translation by Seagull Books, 2025

ISBN 978 1 80309 505 9

British Library Cataloguing-in-Publication Data
A catalogue record for this book is available from the British Library

Typeset by Seagull Books, Calcutta, India
Printed and bound by WordsWorth India, New Delhi, India

To Miro

CONTENTS

THE WATER ANOMALY

1

I was born as an animal, that is if fish
can be considered animals. Eight silver scales
sloughed off me and changed into coins, as
I'd turned into something between a snake woman and
another animal.

Disgusting, murky water wasn't enough for me, I had
to swim away. I'll miss it, the murkiness, the monstrous dusk.

I collect my coins and swim away;
to pay first, and then be something of a snake, a scaly woman,
a frog, a gloominess, a cubic
animal that wounds
with a toothless mouth.

Author's note: The water density anomaly refers to the unusual property of water where its density increases as it cools, but after reaching 4°C, it decreases as it freezes, causing ice to float on liquid water.

BUDDHA

Pale face, white
as a stone at the bottom of a river.
White as a bone
Frida from her self-portrait, in the period
when she painted wild
red backdrops.

You're only a shape, you've got no will.
The gods must be fed,
those dumb children waiting for you, noiselessly;
you won't get rid of them.
Bring him oranges,
sweet rice cakes,
sacred wine.
A black streak of blood flows from his finger.
Sitting here in front of you
oblivious to the point of derangement.
Paper pleas fall from the sky,
they rub their edges against each other,
they bloom and bud, they try
to bear fruit.

He doesn't even move, that challenger of the void,
that pale face
lily pad on the water.

CALDARIUM

The boy with the face of a twenty-year-old Christ
has entered the heated place and at once begun to sweat.
His young, pliant, trembling body of an ancient god
like a statue
covered with the mosaic a hot net makes, an ardent ornament.
And who sculpted him, what generations of mothers,
running to the yard in the very early morning,
between potato drills and bleeding every month
under the worm-eaten logs
of ancient pergolas;
mothers with numbed faces, with snapping mouths
full of wrinkles and squawks, irritable
and basic in their everyday worries; their cry
mixed with the crowing of the roosters, a desolate operetta?

The boy first walked in the mud through the sopping garden,
and in his soul there was a peace gifted to him by nature,
he strolled through his childhood like a martyr who didn't know
he was a martyr, plunging his feet into the mud,
the squelch of his footsteps sounding like an ancient,
village anthem that repeats every
peevish morning:

I know only this world, I invoke only this world,
only into this hot, crowing world was I born,
hens standing by my cradle, and I shared with only them
their diphtheria, pasteurellosis, haemophiliac rhinitis

and chicken lice; and yet I'm happy, even if I already know,
even if in my twenties I already know what winter is,
what hot is, what mothers are and what injustice is.

And therefore young and strong with an imaginary lute on
    my knee
I happily presume to enter
the caldarium; my future world
without feathered operettas, without desperate hens
and without fear.

TEPIDARIUM

I entered the tepidarium, radiant
dry air wafted over me as in childhood,
when I entered the chicken coop with respect and awe
as if into the sacred, foreign territory of a subjugated nation,
where reality twisted in its unsettled
infinity; the warmth and smell of chickens, shavings
smelling of eggs, ordinary, pulsing life and in the air
floating germs where I felt
excited and fulfilled by breaking a ban; that feeling,
that I could do it, be myself in the mystery of the chicken coop,
explorer of an underground underworld, out of sight
of Mother, so close to the strange world,
to those mysterious clucking creatures, so close
to essence.

Something ticked in the chickens' bodies like a good, old,
honest clock, the name of which comes from the Old Slavonic
'to feast': they feasted on plain grain, as I
feasted on this secret experience; hours as such
took on a completely different meaning, hanging from the trees
    in the garden,
gravid pears, at every twitch
of a butterfly wing swelling with their yellow! And beside them
a rusty barrel lying prone, an alluring
submersible and further ban in one; we could only smell the
    odour

of rust, unconsciously recalling to ourselves that we, too,
     would smell
like this one day, when time wraps us in its cocoon, a hoop
still desirous of its own utility, yet already
in the embrace of a loving rust departing without pain into
     nothingness.

I entered the tepidarium to meet myself
with all forms of my own life:
at the same moment I was also a child, entering with awe
the chicken coop; even as a young, frightened boy, shyly
     reaching
for my hot, also forbidden sex; as a man, too,
clueless in the plucked feathers of inexorable maturity,
     reeking of the blood
of slaughtered chickens, the days falling out of me one after
     another
like eggs released from a hen's body just before,
even just after its slaughter, the last continuation of life
after life; as an old man, too, hooped
by the last odour of his own rust.

FRIGIDARIUM

I made love with a woman from an unknown tribe all night long.
I met her by chance by the valley cave, the nape of her neck
glittering with beads of sweat as she bent in the heat
over cowrie shells from which she made necklaces. One of them
chinked together with silver coins also in her abundant
cleavage, each of the coins—a lustful gob of moon spit.
Her hair was covered in a chequered turban, one end of the cloth
flowing down her dark brown back, the lurking tail of an
     innocent chameleon.
She attracted me. She attracted me like the insides of the
     animals I dissected in my youth,
bent over a wooden table; with a secret light suspended
in wicker baskets. Candles dangled above my makeshift
dissection workplace, swayed by a fan; they cast flickers of light
into the innards of the tiny little bodies, where I rummaged
through intestines, eggs and stomachs with impatient fingers.
I never had enough: a body as a box of inaccessible treasure
it lured and tormented by the bestial stink, the matter-of-
     factness of existence,
by the brazen being of a woodwose exhibited for wonder. Grab
     it. Grab it quickly
and avidly, a few cuts, and the theatre of travelling acrobats had
     already begun to roll.
Ferocious medieval dances of people, sicked out from their own
     homes,
that was the squelching of guts for me. I had much to do

not to start licking, smelling and smearing myself with them;
     perversion
and science copulated in my brain like unchaste friends,
     infusing me
with fever
and shame.

I didn't expect the woman with the cowrie shells to welcome
my furtive touches under the teak tree. She accepted my
     importuning
with the matter-of-factness of the monsoon demi-goddess.
     Her acceptance
freed the shame that had been squirming in me as a parasite
     for many years; her love
brought me back to myself in wild, regular waves.

In the morning I bathed in the cold ocean; I became a boy
     again
the moment its water licked my body like a forgiving dog.

A DOG BEING

I have a dog being with me, another
sensibility. It's not so easy
to get into its brain. A cough
puts me at a loss for words, luckily.
I cough words like bad luck.

I'm at a loss for (in) words, I just want to go
into a dog's brain, into another sensibility.

So that I could be
a beautiful handmaid, a priestess
of dog sensibility; in a cave full of dog being, dog hurt.
In the sanctuary of a pure,
trusting brain.

SNAIL

A spiral, an endless snail,
a snail that has awoken, that sleeps,
that senses
and about which we know nothing.

Snaa-snaa, says the snail.
Slime-slime, it replies.

I feel life through its saliva
as it slides upwards
without a single necessary

thought of heaven.

IN RED

I can't sleep in the still house
on the hot August night, filled
with warning signs,
strange flowers erupting from the bed
glowing in the dark.
Come to me, stranger, let me
smell your hair
For that I'll give you

the delirious dark of my body,
its lunar red, dreamlike
and cursed. Take off your hat, take off your boots
with spurs, enter,

drink wine, eat
a piece of a slaughtered beast

and then deliver me from memory
in one swift movement.

AMONG THE ROSE HIPS

Among the rose hips, among the blackberries
a slippery stone in the hollow under my throat.
He put it there, his hundred hands
having just covered my impatient body
like huge beetles swarming
hungrily—without its juices
they'd have shrivelled, they'd have remained
just plain and simple wing cases.
Among the rose hips, among the raspberries
with my head in the net of a local sun,
I fall obligingly
to the rediscovered grass.

On the wide table of the forest
all manner of food, joy
is born and hatched in a thousand
forms; gentle postcards,
responsive invitations
from moss emanate to me.

Among the rose hips, among the bushes
my body calms down, for a moment
open, then closed
in known, in forgotten
rhythms,

Here sleeps one, happy, alive,
a spring bubbling in my arms, in my legs.

NAKEDNESS

Nakedness like a white whip
snaps about the flat, winged horses
and knickers are inapt, there's just
plain and simple
nakedness, a bare wall with a shadow.
Knees, pale sugar cubes,
bait for felt-coated
dormice, erupting
from the dark. Bras and feathers
from peacock and baboon, the honey
of an arm. Unhurriedly and completely
poured papaya; furs

and dead grapes. Nakedness
clicks her teeth, blusters

with embryos and childbirth,
with over-ripeness

and emptiness.

OPIUM POPPY

Pleasure once more; I want to say
a few words about your body. It doesn't depend
on language. Abroad
loses its adamant face, becomes
a tamed animal, and you
are an excellent gift, a satisfaction.
A cult of the body, a taunt
from the present; and yet charming
this wordless statement: your muscles, a bouquet
of silent fireworks, cords
in your forearm; skin, warm
like a stream-crossed wetland, with crowfoot
and the smell of clay, here and there
opium poppy. Seasons
of your body: you can gaze
up into the sky, spread wide
your grateful arms;

savouring,
submitting,
a wild horse, galloping
from the depths of your throat.

BLUE GAP

The last night with you, the wine almost
drunk up, its red breath
still damp. The Thai music
lies like an embryo in a dark womb
in this enchanted, craved-for
room. Is it the scent that's shackled me to you,
Blue Gap, mingled with the odour
of musty books? I touch you
for the last time, like my mother in childhood
killing a rooster; he's lovely still
and yet already gone. The wine is improper,
like blood, it shouldn't be here. It shines, a pomegranate
full of pips, a derisive
ruby.

The indefinite pain, known as dailiness,
comes with a dog's licked face, with the dog
howling. We sleep entangled in one another, but
from my breast a fantastical
red eye gazes at you,

unwavering it waits as if the coming morning
wouldn't wound it with some

useless scrap of a glass lens from the heavens.

BRAIN DEATH

Today suddenly in the light
I looked at my body. Criss-crossed by cat paws,
naked and pink it seemed to me like a piece of meat.
Heavy breasts I no longer need; a bum,
which looks to me reflected in glass
like a personal insult. But what's inside!
The flesh is a marvellous pink
just inside. Everything Works. From inside
It is the Unlooked For Beauty with which
I've never dealt.

Life comes from within. Living
I'm from the depths. Wasted breath teaching you that in school;
    my brain,
if a tram passed over it, would be like a piece
of annoying mud. Old and grey—
a wet sheet of paper.
Did someone write on it serious, passionate
confessions? They'd crumble in a shriek
from people passing by when they'd see it. Wretched
brain, discarded scrambled eggs; scattered under a tram.
They'd watch. It would be me.

But my brain, trampled to pieces,
would still live on there. It would be raining,
people shouting; the brain would recall for a while after death

unexpected details. Memories of a body, pinked
with cat scratches; memories
of love which really happened. There a wedding dress,
there childbirth, studies; indifference.

MECHANICAL DOLL

I'm a mechanical doll. So you set me up.
Just for you I played for three months
this so many times hackneyed,

sorry,

this simple, containing just a few notes,
tacky melody of a cat in heat. A melody
of unending orgasms. There are, alas, more

than poems and education. Orgasm,
a taboo lure; this female

ultimately anatomical
not quite explicable, always other, always
elusive;

culturally and historically
so often inadmissible;

tantalizing and shrouded in legend,
like the fable about the woman who as a seal came out of
    the sea
and made love to a man
who tore her in two

like fire and knife,
flayed the skin from her body and forced her to be
what she couldn't.

I also wanted to be
for you what I couldn't.

A mechanically dancing doll
in a red velvet bra
lifting up her artificial, insensate arms
at the bottom of a bottle of golden alcohol,

to the sounds of a melody
containing just a few simple notes.

I'm a woman who at the same time is a man.
Because I'm a woman, I want to own the man that I am.
Because I'm a man, I want to own the woman
that I am. Because I'm the woman, whom the man that I am
wants to own, I run away from him.
Because I'm a woman, I'm not in control.
Because I'm a woman, he second-guesses me.
Because he second-guesses me, I defend myself.
I defend myself as a woman. As a man, too.
Because I'm a man, bloody wounds remain
on my body. Because I'm a woman, they remain on me likewise
on my heart.

Because I'm a woman, I lick them.
Because I'm a man, I'm silent about all this destruction.
Because I'm a man, I depart from myself; I get out.

Because I'm a woman, I've got no choice, just to wait;
or leave as well. The second
is harder.

I-BEAST

The I-beast comes into the room, looks around
and finds only
tatters of my night, my body, my hands
and the flies that have died
on the bed sheet.
Tatters of a body that spoke so much
idly,
of a night that tormented
with sleeplessness like a three-hundred-year plague,
of hands that have aged
in direct light, reflected
in the mirror's aggression,
flies that have left shaming traces
after their small, insignificant lives.

The I-beast tells me something, but
I don't hear it any more, I don't know what it is
and why it comes to the scraps
of what used to be me;
a last moan conveyed
to the shell of my ear
its distant calling: I-beast!
I-beast————————

and it seems to me that it is about love; but
could be

likewise about killing.

Bring me water, a man calls
across a garden full of wild grass,
the brooding sun having battered his lips, sucked dry
hidden springs, lured out, avid juices,
sweat, the deep, concealed
reservoirs of moisture. The air has trembled
with hallucinatory heat, poppies and dahlias,
huge as pies of meadow dragons, with gaping
mouths confronting the day, brave, strong,
ridiculous. There are moments when in the body
pretexts rise fragile and unguarded,
like froth bull's spit,
that compel you trembling
to give way to frenzied colours, in like state
to move around the house unconsciously,
drinking emerald wine from the womb of round bottles,
     touching the walls;

to creep over the terrace, watching
through a secret night window
on to a pair in a room
laughing bewitchingly
her brown body a fiery tomboy's
like an ornament without clothes, a promise till dawn,

oh, this island, this wild grass
this insanity, jealousy;
let the ground crack beneath my feet
by morning and from it sprout
the deviltree.

YOU AND ME WHEN THE COCK CROWS

It's incomprehensible, that border of yours
between the feverish night and the healing morning; as if you
    didn't recognize
the differences between frenzied hyacinths and tamed hyenas.
    What you tell me
in the evening, no longer applies in the morning, and vice versa:
    like a fisherman you drag
a boat repaired a hundred times, wrecked in his fury, despair
    and at the bellowing
predatory water. Like a drunken fisherman
you drag me, a hundred-times repaired illusion of love, a crazy
closeness, a hollow shell with a mushy inside, scratched
and patched up again in the desire to possess what is yours, in
    the desire not to let be possessed
what is yours, no one else's; in the desire to immure the devil in
    the wall
and again skin your hands down to black blood, while
    destroying the plaster, while tearing down
the walls. Don't cry darling, my love, I'm with you. Ah, my sore,
    jealous hands
will again build an airy room, not just a room, a castle
propped up with the leg of a magpie.

THE CRY OF THE PEACOCK

Sometimes a bitter fruit, a fruit of bitter berries
breaks in upon your love after which only
a flimsy envelope of darkness arrives. Then
you rest your cooling head on the table waiting
so the nearest tree in the garden holds out its layered
sleeves to you through the window.

Over the scrubbed tiles run
little mourning folk, those who lived with you
in the garden house; each a completed, round year
strung on a thread like a gem. Wear it proudly, with the face
of a former goddess, recall the times when you awoke
always with a new baby in your womb, over and over
picking over the secrets of fertility, beans,
white and black.

Continue to sit at the clean table, look for water
in the depth of crystal balls; let the wind, let it untangle
your hair, once more to be like the pelt of a foal, light brown
     and delicate.

And don't start up when sometimes in sleep
you hear the pitiless cry of a peacock: it's only your dead love

hailing you from the night.

Timotej took the bird, whose life
I wished to save. I put the bird in his hands
with trust. Its legs had to be bound so it could be pricked
with an injection. To care for him humanely, in a friendly way.
    Timotej
took it in his huge hands, spread its wings and said
Leave it to me. My family looked at him
and applauded.

He spread its wings and pinned one to the board,
on which it lay. Uselessly,
I screamed. He had a bowl of water there, on which
the wing rested and blood began to flow into the water: minute,
the blood of a bird. The water was pink. I ran away
because there was no escape.

I got on a bus.
Suddenly there was an earthquake, and I, with a bird's terror,
with a horror of Timotej, still ran away. But the bus
stopped. Sitting in front of me was a man in an orange coat.
He had a pocket at the back and another man was sitting in
    front of him who (unintentionally?)
let fall the rubber belt that was supposed to protect him.

The belt blasted, tearing the pocket of the man in front of me,
as the earthquake went on. The rubber belt shot out

so that it hurt my ear. Until then I'd been closely
watching the man sitting in front of me; he was in agony
and bleeding. Everyone shouted. They scolded me
that I didn't know how to live, that I couldn't save even the tiniest
living being.

The rubber belt had whacked me in the head; the man in front
    of me
was squirming with pain. All at once blood splashed
and I raised my hand to where my ear flapped. I didn't feel
the man's agony.

I only recall as I bent
over him and looked for things. A bag
and computer. Everything was covered in clotted blood
and they all shouted, go on, get out

and then wash your hands. In case you catch another bus.
And don't kill a bird again.

PORTRAIT OF THE LATE MRS PARTRIDGE

This woman looks like the embodiment of lightning, her red
hair grows from the nape of her neck, pointing upwards,
     towards the turbulent
sky. Her scarlet clothes have a wide skirt
in the shape of a partridge. She holds a mystical cauldron
like some Ceridwen from the past,
one moment she looks like a hen, one moment a greyhound,
the setting sun shining through her head, a flamingo!
even a few days before death! —and yet she's had enough of
     loving
on rotten fruit, enough twilit hills, autumnal litanies.

The master of the house had commissioned me; I took a
     long journey
to them, I was pickled to the gills, staring
at the torpor of the gravel. She opened to me majestically;
     her legs
under her velvet dress in flat shoes, on her head a hat
with fruit and stuffed birds. Whole nights
we talked through, relaxed in the attic, at noon
we began work so that in the evening again and again
from earthenware vessels we'd sip the wine,
trickling down our haunches.

I painted her as best I knew how:
purple and blue on her partridge skirt, scorn in her eyes,

and humour; yes, I even allowed myself to put humour in
    the portrait,
under the old man's nose. She could never
truly belong to me: the beauty of her young Malay goddess face
is lost in the small details next to the skirt, unimportant
in the flood of orange hair, in the bushy luxuriance of her dress.

Yes, I desired to wound her with an image, to defeat the
sarcasm and mystery of her gaze; put more fire into things,
than into her: what happened, indeed is not my fault, after the
    work was done
I departed as requested.

Since then I have painted many paintings. In the galleries
they've displayed so many that one can't even look at them;
    I became
famous, celebrated as an old madrigal. In my courtyard
children are playing, a woman with a sonorous voice is hanging
    out laundry.
I stand in an attic room, looking at a painting, the portrait
the late Mrs Partridge returns scorn to me: her hair irradiated
    by fire
I see even through the flames that consume it, I see her eyes,
as I saw them then, a torch, tumbling from the roof.

THE BODY OF THE LATE MRS PARTRIDGE

Suddenly this red flower opened, I'd watched it
already for a few days, but without fully concentrating. I
    suddenly saw it
from above. Essentially I thought it wasn't there;
that it was there without existence, just like that.
Only a red flower, perhaps a traveller or a worm,
or scarlet, met on the way.

But it opened like a gaping mouth, tongue sticking out.
I took fright from it because it was bending from the fires and
    things like that. Because of the dreadful explosion, I forgot
    the eyes in it, in that flower:
eyes,
of which I otherwise take care. From the outside
they aren't as attractive as a few years ago, and for that reason
have they improved for me? Will everything of which I don't
    take care improve?

I want to digress, not
to watch, I want to go underground, to a passage
there, to cool safety, not embrasures,
not underground hiding places from gunfire. This grey-haired
    man
sneaks up on me, but I don't respond. Until now
I've tried to respond to everyone.

That red flower flashed out like a crazy pinafore.

I was, alas, in the middle of it. There
I burned, with a purple, fleshy heart
incomparable with anyone or anything; with a plain and
    simple body.

Nothing about why.

THE DEATH OF MRS PARTRIDGE

Not really a long marriage, bearing in mind
youth appearance. In the mirror I saw
dark eyes; red hair untouched anywhere
by a layer of dye, it flowed from my head
like a torrent of unconscious words.

I was born
under a blackberry bush, half-Malay,
half-Irish. We travelled the world,
so many languages that I took on
and men, I took them like pills.
In Hawaii in a white house with stone
adornments on the walls, in Japan on straw
mats, in Mauritius in a bath of flowers, and so on.

The old man bought me, his sudden love,
a lake, I the boat. He braided vines
into my hair curling from its grip to the water's surface,
a wedding veil full of expectations.

He shouldn't have summoned the young painter so that my
    image
would convey my passion; and colours. The optical illusion
of our liaison broke in the harsh light changing
in the afternoons, his magical hands, under whose touch
my blood breathed, suffused to bursting.

I was a fruit, a stuffed bird. At length
he forced himself to go, yet I don't know what drove him
    out, I stayed
with an old man who loved me like no other.

I don't remember who threw the match
into a pile of old silk sheets
and tippets in the tower. The blackberry
simply burst; disgorged blackness.

THE HUSBAND OF THE LATE MRS PARTRIDGE

The woman seemed familiar to me
and at the same time suicidal like a blind poppy.
She had the lightning of a knife, a hydra
in a soft wrapping. I was fascinated by how she held her
    head—
as if at any moment it would be placed on the block on the
    gallows—,
inclined at a certain angle, calling forth images of torture:
to seize her and tie her to a chair, bind her hair
even hands with sailor's knots! To put icicles of honey in her
    mouth,
watch them flow down her translucent throat, to subdue her;
teach her my speech, absolute submission.

Love like an impatient, sticky tongue burst from my guts,
on the way to her womb, flies latching on to it,
delirious friends from the portals of hell, and word-galls,
    ominous,
swollen balls of grapes. I hated her for her glamour
with which she held me in thrall. For making me feel
    unceasing hunger for her,
gluttony and lust; for addiction and envy which
she cast at my feet as tantalizing gifts.

I wanted to own her forever, Ishtar of Mesopotamia.
Her portrait would hang above my bed so that I'd constantly
see it, her colourful skirt would burn my face
day and night, until the violent, scent of dawns
scorching.

THE LATE MRS PARTRIDGE'S WAKE

I've returned secretly to the wake to drink a toast
of sparkling wine with the bereaved. What rich tables,
pewter glasses shine in the light of candles and fire from the
    hearth,
on the table in my honour partridges stuffed with figs,
smoked pigeons, pease pudding with beans, sticky conserves
and mussels, St James' scallops. Sitting at the tables are
darkened figures resembling crows in the form of undertakers,
whispering something to each other, the terrifying details
of their stories hover over the tables like curses.
I haven't noticed if among them there is also something of mine.

A man sits at the top table, his face,
wrinkled from the tertiary era, with an incalculable expression.
The atmosphere is gloomy, but still audible
is a ubiquitous slurping, gurgling and belching,
as if the whispered stories haven't had as much power
as unstoppable bodily hunger and thirst.

Then an outcry is heard in the air:
at first seeming like hysteria, the sobs of a drunken woman;
later turning into laughter. It rises cascading
up to the dome, leaping in various tones
up an aerial stair, vibrates and writhes,
a reeling entity floating to the heavens.

The others hesitantly join in: the contagiousness of laughter,
inappropriate and relaxing, a local band playing,
bare feet stomping and skirts twirling, cymbals clash
and dulcimers and bagpipes, someone shooting sparklers
    into the window,
sweaty couples spinning on the stone floor, on the hearth
purring like an amiable cat;
and my eyes light up as then
even through death I feel the fire within me, shooting out
    into the night.

CIRCE

My eyes drop down to the water, a rare
moment of settling on a stone bowl brings me
grief. In vain I drew my bow, sharpened
my arrow tips, bloodied my mouth with berries: he left, but
    not before
he snatched the strength from me, the shoulder on which he
    leaned. Memories
prevent immobility: he appeared, bright head
wreathed with greenery sprouting from the earth's centre—
out of nowhere he stirred within me, oh yes, a demigod
of delight. It was sweet
to slip into weakness, the witchcraft
of animals, into games—it was joyful
turning the unneeded into swine, debauching
the juice of pomegranates from the clefts
of his body, to bind him
with my braids. But at night

I saw women in his dreams, my restless
heart moved away from me. On my thighs
small snakes crawled upwards, with a quiet
rustle they lifted the night fabric of my dress, sliding
up the hips to my breasts, where
they slept. I protected myself with sleeplessness: I cast a spell
on his dreams against those of his in the palms of his hands,
    before morning

I smeared him with a mixture of saliva and anger, snake
oozings.

He left: I was left with only malice, a cave full
of bubbling ingredients. However, he carries
in the folds of his skin poison, mixed
for all the bodies of his women: after love with him
from them they will be

my sisters.

WILDSISTER

She looks at me, she
who returns from the night, her cheeks
throbbing in the distance, in her wrists
sadness. Half-alive,
half-dead, bewitched,
cursed,
on both hips a knife—
on one side water, on the other
blood.
Dressed-undressed,
in her mouth crying and singing,
she returns down the slope
to home-not-home.

She knows: under the trees it rains twice,
she knows: death edges from the walls, can toll the bell
at any time.

She returns, my wild sister.
Neither on foot nor in a wagon,
on her shoulder an owl, in her hand
an apple, in her apple
love, in her love
poison.

WILDBROTHER

Untroubled animals run through his head,
which he lets go when hunting. His hands,
hot as well-tempered instruments,
clasped on my body, kindle within me
secret fires. He tries not to see
a pupil of free sin
in my narrowed eyes. He accepts me.
He accepts the phantasmagorias which afflict me
night after night. Accepts my shallowness, rage,
menstruation; days when I retreat into myself
traces of unremoved mascara on the pillow,
on the hollows of my fully developed,
difficult womanhood.

He is only here for me. He gazes,
biting unbearably into me, as my
womanhood rolls from me hand to hand, a cocoon, gravid
with something that can't be guessed in advance; until bursting
swollen by its unpredictability.

He smells ravenangelically, ravenstagdeer incest. He smells
of flayed rabbit pelt; blood. He smells of everything
that I could be if
once I'd been born as him.

Wildbrother; painful twin with whom
I sleep.

VIRGINIA

She filled the pockets of a long brown dress with stones,
two black braids lining ears behaving so calmly!
There's nothing like her head, she's silent, divulging
neither rustle nor scent. All her thoughts
are already stacked like ancient cards side by side,
arranged according to a prehistoric calendar, according to a
      priceless book,
the only one left here from ancient times.
I sense the watery eye's attention.
Oh, it's already absent, ahead of time, as when fantasy
      extends a step
to its owners, talks to fish. I, too, can open my mouth
      like that,
like you, whole books I've opened with an empty mouth,
      o, o, o, o, o, and thus
whole pages. So I would like to make at least some sound
      with them. Up to my knees
I'm already in cold water, now a strange mass will move to
      my guts,
enter my vagina and fill me inside, coldness and emptiness
      and wet,
I'll feel like some kind of mushroom, growing out of
      moisture and rotting
in moisture, as if moisture were an omnipresent, maternal
      power, primordial,

fore-mother, fore-sister and fore-cosmos. The water is
    already nearing my heart, its blue part
becoming ever bluer. I'm dying in the blue, in a moment
    my veins
will colour and transform, and the water is already in my
    ears, it's already licking my calm braids
like a faithful dog. I'll try to keep my eyes open when I'm
    flooded, I'll still
try to get some aquatic animal wings, and then once more
    rise up, once more
to float.

I sense the watery eye's attention.
From the lake's cathedral I hear bassoons.
And suicide is just a superstition.

THREE YOUNG WOMEN ARE PLAYING DICE

Three young women are playing dice
in the sleepy light of the lamp, in a room
a ghostly dead-alive. On the table black calamari
and lobsters, rended with their pink mouths,
reminiscent
of a voracious feast of witches.
They sip spiced wine, it runs down the creases of their
    cheeks
and bellies to their thighs. They banish boredom
by reading hallucinatory books; they paint their palms
with blackened lipsticks, greasy circles
from pheasant soup they scry as in voodoo.

In a house with almost no light, around the roof of which
bats fly, behind the flickering of the fire, in the room,
with a smell of bitter currants, darkening
like the nipples of an old woman's breasts,
with the screeching
of night birds, with the birth of frogs

three young women are playing dice.

NECROMANCER

On the counter with a painting of an animal, something
        between a dormouse and a bear,
giant robin eggs have been laid. Azure-blue, ready for juggling
acrobatics. In a tube shaped like a bubble an embryo of
        an animal
sublimates, something between a small bear and a small
        dormouse. In the bubble
new bubbles are forming.

A black and white figure with the face of a kite and fish eyes
is standing by the counter looking at me. For a long time he has
        convinced me that I'm
Dead. But *I'm* not dead, the rest of *you are*! Finally, he begins
to toss those robin eggs, *helicobacter necromancer*,
I'm your only audience if you want some applause.

The necromancer peels away from the wall, his robes fluttering
        across the room
like an executioner's cloak, throwing glittering circles into the
        sky's marquee, humming to himself
a melody 'Medusa, you robbed me of my youth.' This show
is performed exclusively for me. We have been living together
        for a long time
in this house, he having moved here when the walls whitened
        and the last
birds from the neighbourhood had flown away. I hear him
        at night

tap a secret crutch down the stairs, then descend
into the darkness of the garden, at the end of which is a creek.

Several times I've watched him sitting among the wet
trees, legs in the dark water, rod in hand. Only then
do I feel a pity about which he doesn't know. Then
he's suddenly different: an absurd, black-and-white hood
folded in his lap, rubbing his fish eyes, staring
beyond the bay; for a moment there is a truce
between us, similar to peace. I leave him like this

and return to the house. I sleep until morning, almost
happy. In the morning I make out on the fence
the oddities he's caught: a four-armed monkey, a longwinged
butterfly-moth, all kinds of lepidoptera, dried fish stomachs,
pages of old books.

In the afternoon we play cards—every time I lose
he laughs throatily, and starts again with that hackneyed vinyl:
We live here because you're Dead. You think that you aren't,
   but the opposite
is the truth. But I'm not dead, the rest of you are!

In an atmosphere of anger we await the evening when for me
he puts on a show. First he stands at the counter
with a painting of an animal that is something between a bear
   and a dormouse, then
he starts juggling.

And then another music creeps into the house, transparent as a
   dragonfly's wing,
descends on the stage, touches

the black and white cloak; and all at once it doesn't depend
    on who is dead or why;
it depends on this music, on robin eggs,
on dream acrobatics, on different colours
exploding into the night.

CENTAUR

The centaur with a mysterious, wild body,
blackened by night music, with the look
of abandoned crows at the end of November, approaches
my house, in his mouth a silver
harmonica. He calls me out, the centaur does, dribbles
glittering spit, winds its threads like a web
round the corners of my autumn dwelling, impatiently
tosses his head and pants behind the windows, a centaur
without time, without the will to wait,
without face.

So many times was I
ready to go out into the garden dusk,
to touch his chest, gaze at his dark profile;
so many times hidden in the heavy folds of the curtains,
did I watch him, how he shook his hips, how
his harmonica cast gleams of starlight
on his thick-haired sex.

Only at the moment I yield myself to the mercy of his arms,
    am I covered
by shadows of the strange vaults that accompany him,
after his kiss I feel in my mouth
the taste of ginger and a dreadful forest, from my palm he
    carefully
bites out a pearl;

I return disordered, without the will
to wait, without time; like an eternal spider
I begin from within to spin around my house

with dark saliva.

And then they saw the Minotaur's daughter. She sat there,
    on a solitary chair,
with her noble, horned head in her hands and a red dress.
    Neither cheerful
nor even sad, she just stared into space; at times she acted
    like a visitor,
that had walked into the house insouciantly as a queen, not
    caring if anyone had invited her.
She was sitting in the living room.

The two boys watched her from behind the long tablecloth.
    Two little,
well-behaved boys—somewhere between childhood and doubt,
between the desire to obey and to scramble into a hedge and
    from there
try whether bad things work the way they should. The way
    they imagine.

There were long white columns in the living room that served
    instead of a window. From the outside
pressed inwards a steel-grey darkness, scored with some
    unknown handwriting.
A huge white figure loomed in the middle of the living room,
    but differently
from the Minotaur's daughter, it had just blown in there.
    In a corner there danced
the Spirit of a dancer and the dogs, too, were white.

Behind the long tablecloth, the two boys deliberated what to
    say. What to say
to the daughter of the Minotaur, who'd visited them with all
    those attendant visitors.
At length they decided not to say anything: they just listened
to the black music of Nightwish, to the sounds of the wind-
    like dancing in the folds of the clothes
of everyone present, to the murmur
of a fallen rose, lying on the floor, to the rattling
of glass balls which were all over the place.

They stood there and just watched her. This somewhere
between childhood and doubt
scratched deep in their throats.

RAVENANGEL

Every night
he comes to me with laborious
wings, drenched with rain. I make a place
for him in my bed, on my thighs feeling
the coldness of his embrace; I strive
to hug his sable-sad head to my breast.
It takes me so long to become used to the burden, which
he grants me as a gift, it takes so long to warm
my solitary legs. With resignation
my pale skin accepts the transparent moistness of water,
of a ravenangel's sperm and spit. Who's to say where he
        wanders when
night has fallen; what might have happened to him, cast out
not of his own will into the horror of life. I forgive him
this coldness, this wetness, relieved
of my daily grind I accept everything,
I pity;
I try to feel his
pulse, to stroke
his exhausted nape.

He brings me nothing, except slimy
different stinks offering sleep,
except traces of bitter-tender efforts through which
he hopes to overcome futility
and the night.

In the morning I find by my head
a shed grey feather. I draw a bath,
slowly, as when they lower on thick ropes
into a grave a last
posthumous rose as I open
a window.

The ravenangel regards me
from the wilderness of the day;

even at midday I sense in me
our mutual,
black children pushing forward

into relentless life.

RAVENANGEL II

The toothless black child in me
tried to smile but to no avail.
Its faint smile became a sneer, the grimace
of an unwanted foetus. Its contorted face inclined
to one side and wept. It cried horribly within me, shaking
all over its wrinkled, unlovely body, it sobbed
in my guts, it wailed
intolerably tossing and turning
in a fever all that long, rainy night, when morning
was long gone from view and the moon
walked among the rocks of Montserrat and pricked
     everything with barbs,
that seemed to be still alive.

The toothless ravenangel baby was bleeding in my
     blackened womb
all that long night. We wept together
for three endless days until it finally emerged from me
along with a clot of dried blood
as with a greeting from those who wanted so much to live,
until they cried themselves into an eternal, hypnotic sleep,

and until I buried him
like a tiny kitten with a star on its afflicted brow
under a dry, black, barren
tree.

55

He passed a grey wing across my face, a membrane,
which, veined, half covered his face like a veil.
Why aren't you my brother, I asked him.
The light shone only in the fields,
as if the fireflies were playing hide and seek,
casting their inconsequential glow between the furrows
and the evening disinterred itself in clumps from the hollows.

I'm not your brother, for your time has yet to come.
You can't rejoice, because sorrow still endures.
Don't expect a new tale because the old one has yet to finish.

UNDER THE SNOW

Under the snow is another world; all the passions
have burrowed into the ground like moles
fleeing from the light.
Colours expand on the horizon,
camouflage. Such silence!
And meanwhile swirling under the snow,
ground water currents twisting there,
setting
traps of lake beasts.
The bark of trees seems to sleep
concealing a secret sap. The winter birds
know this, falling upon the snow
like curses.

It won't last long now. Slender fingers of grass
will clamber upwards
firmly gripping the earth.
A blind spring
roams through the underground labyrinth; it's
that lurking pain,
loops of dark promises.

OWL

It's required to fear owls: because they inherit
two souls. Their two souls mean
four lives. The owl is two-fold: eerily
symmetrical, each half of its face
appearing double in the mirror
and each one different. When it spreads its dark wings,
a mantle of rain is laid upon the earth
and its shadow reflected there
like a Picasso cube. The owl
is cubic. It cubes and koobs into the night calling
koo, a bloodthirsty koom-doomsayer.

It's required to fear owls: they'll get under your fingernails,
dig into your hair, thieve your soul,
and you'll live with their claws forever
on your nape, doubled by owls and broken in two,
held together only by their four lives.
None of them will ever be yours.

BATS

Just look how they can define themselves, as if
they didn't even get any of the plans
for the filigree work of the Creator. In the glassy darkness
they catch hold of each other's dangling hands,
tender embryos,
twins, quintuplets.
repeated a hundred, a thousand times,
a tireless pattern of teeny-weeny innards, modelled
in the hope that they immediately after birth become
souvenirs of the world. Unrepeatable.
Only for the Unrepeatable. Only for the light
which looks down upon us, sent secretly from on high,
to be delighted in

by this miracle on the walls of a cave.

CAT

Emerges suddenly like music. Comes from who knows where
dragged by the wild gusts of the past night,
bats squatting in her fur.
Calm, evil eyes focused on you, waiting,
for you to speak. But what should I say to her
how can I converse with her about loneliness, about death,
     when she,
queen of black curtains, actress, knows everything
and more. I lose myself
in her ironic silence, so much put
behind her. Multicoloured as the wind
appears and she regards me: what do her serpentine
     movements wish
to tell me, has she come to console?
Hardly. At least she acts as though she participates. No one will
     find out
the secret of her bowels, about the fizzing brain that drives her
once forward, once there where she nests.
Wise and derisive, requests nothing. If only for me at least
she'd play a cat march on a granny's rosary,
scratch her halloos on the window glass.
Yet she just gazes. Star-born friend;

I wept all over
her silk coat.

POEM FOR THE EYES OF A DOG

Dog eyes that glow in my sky
I beg you to stay and watch
over my strange dreams today and tomorrow.
I walk through the sombre garden, cap
over my ears, in my soul whispering
an Our Father for dogs, for myself and for you, and my fear
seems less.

You've taught me a lot
about light and dark, about simple things.
Since I've known you, there's no place in me any more
for complicated prayers. Just look, the earth

drives out young trees, they stretch to the sky like threads
and they tug the sky back to earth. And in between
love—nothing more
nothing less.

BIRDBATH

An undertaker bird and a white-haired priest in a big black hat
are bathing a pelican. The undertaker bird has a human form,
     all wrapped up
in (black) mummy-style bandages. In its hands a (white) rag,
his job is to rub, wipe, rub, wipe
and wipe. The priest sprays the pelican's face, doing so
with the thoroughness of an alchemist; the pelican crouches in a
     concrete tub
with animal legs. The sky is English, cloudy.
The two are standing outside, wearing autumnal shoes. Beyond
     this scene
is an airy Bird House with two antennae.

Given the setting, the scene could be gruesome.
However, the pelican acts as though the bird bath hasn't
     happened to him for the first time.
His wings are bent in mild shock; he has no choice but
     to endure.
It hasn't even occurred to him that this could also be a last
     anointing.
The undertaker bird and the white-haired priest
enact their roles with a deadly gravity.
All their usual duties have been set aside: with the attention
     of scientists
they bend over the pelican, driven

by some higher power, higher ordinance: with such
    single-mindedness as apparently Hitler's henchmen
    implemented the will of the One in Whom They Believed.
There is also the consistency of the inquisition: spray, rub, wipe,
spray, rub, wipe, spray, rub.

The pelican waits resignedly; after bathing him
they'll apparently take him to the Bird House and leave him
    there. He'll
shake three times, expelling
from his coat the last drops: in his heart
he'll be warmed by the relief of the afflicted; the innocent vanilla
scent of the shampoo.

MY STEP-SISTER'S HEN

My step-sister stands in the middle of the room, wholly
radiant and golden with a serious expression on her face.
    She looks
like an overgrown sun, with the figure of a barmaid or
circus ring leader with a whip. Simply a ring-mistress. The room
is a kerosene blue, outside the window is a row of trees with
    stags and does.

Nonchalantly, as if nothing had happened, she is holding a hen
    on a leash.
The hen comes up to her waist; she has medium long, black
    wavy hair, from anger
she grinds her teeth. Scarlet feathers fall from her as from a
    Japanese maple.

And who said that their relationship couldn't be happy.
    Certainly there are days when
they lie together in a four-poster bed, reading
the daily press and the Pre-Raphaelite poets, when over
    their heads
a dancer, turned upside down, just runs along the ceiling on
    a unicycle.

But now is a moment of defiance. The hen bares her teeth,
    scarlet
is my step-sister's hen, reproving
as fire, obedient despite her own will. Just wait, says the hen.

One day you will be in a collar, as happens between owners
and the owned. One day we will switch roles. I will shine
and you, you will be a little tamed lion; a golden,
step-sister hen.

My step-sister nonchalantly, as if nothing had happened,
pulls the enraged hen to her, leads her into the darkness
of the canopy bed. She selects a daily newspaper
and a book by a Pre-Raphaelite poet; nods to the ceiling, greets
the dancer riding a wall on a unicycle. Fine, says
my step-sister. She kisses the hen
and dowses the occult lamp, flickering into the darkness.

YOSHIKO

In the garden Yoshiko smells the early roses,
the arms of morning entwining her ankles, young snakes, born
in the shades of bushes, in the earth. In the mountains' midst
    just beside
my shuttered window
Yoshiko dwells: beyond the peak
of my oppressive dream
she emerges from her home as if from an egg shell,
gazing, as beneath
her hands the morning buds and blooms, drawing
juice from the earth. Touching the soil
calls forth a trembling in her, joy from the burgeoning
foliage. It mounts up
to her throat until she begins to sing, her clear voice
declaring her taut, bodily
union with the day.
The song comes to my scratchy
straw bed: it entwines about my ankles, a snake,
born from its joy.
I crawl to the shuttered window, through a slit in the wood
I gaze at her, a sad voyeur:
roses nuzzle her
like tame animals. I wonder
as they do; I envy
them warmth, the viviparous

cocktail in their capillaries; I envy Yoshiko
this sensual-bright
liquid vein, which permits her

to survive everything.

THE OLD WOMEN

The old women wearing grey suits, sweaty
former nursemaids, bearers
of snakes and medusas, foster-mothers of bald
teddy bears in their
empty wombs. The old women
without wombs. The old women
who have forgotten: they collect
only what is. Toadstools
and small change, worm notes.

Grey-haired; not our mothers,
not us. High heels
on varicose legs; a face—the posthumous
mask of Marilyn.

That's not us. We still
regularly gaze into the face
of the bloody moon in the toilet
bowl. Youth, you howl
like a dog; you depart

on a very strange road.

JOURNEY

It opens before you as if it shone.
Come, it says. It's so easy to step out
to choose the unknown, there,
where no guilt yet shadows the horizon,
no beloved animal lies dead on the road
and no weeping sky
mourns over him. It's so simple
to pack a few things, not look back
and leave what already has been but
still hurts.

There's movement on the journey.
Your blood will stir again, yes, that harsh-smelling one,
almost dried up, the one that's bothered you
your entire life. Throw to me on the journey
dark rose petals for an older bride:
like her I believe that I can now
breathe, knowing what is required for the journey
to be a journey,
only the journey, and not

approaching something that waits in the distance
like an intricate arabesque that can change
to happiness,
to love,
to death or
whatever you label it

until before your eyes
it dissolves into nothing because that's what
it always was. Come, says the mirage. That's why it's so easy
to pack up and just go.

IKITSUKI ISLAND

Here a huge Buddha sits above two villages,
plump, grey and gazing off into the distance.
Guards, or
he dreams his own. I came here
by raft: I'm a revelation; here they'd yet to see
a fair-haired woman. Children run out
of the houses, on their faces
astonished eyes—huge
coffee cups, cakes
from dark beans, glittering
fish. I reach out from a window—
all at once I've got a hand
in another house. On the clay floor
a smiling woman stands
barefoot, a little of her music
eddies from her hair;

the blood fizzing
in my head. The sea,
embraceable as a dog,
enters the yard.

PORCELAIN

The sun passes through the porcelain, leans
on its rounded edges, a golden egg on a shore
with herons. An unbearable white
tires the eyes and lulls, a round
tablet of oblivion. In just a moment

I'll look into its open
gullet to raise my spirits. The sun will
laugh indifferently, a molten apple
in the middle of snow, at the bottom
of a watching well.

Finally, I fall asleep in porcelain silence,
its coldness getting into my bones
and holding fast—

and the life I've led so far
will ring there like a last coin
and will be just a reflection:
finally, pure, finally mine.

BAMBOOS

They shoot up, irresistible
as a snake. They slip out quick, they slide
out, their tongues scaly and massive. They recall
male secrecy, the vehemence
of fleshly love; likewise
rebellion and fertility.
In vain you gather
the shoots, newly born
children, vainly placing them
on a stony plate: with their roots
they lock hard into the earth, lively from clay
and rain. They burrow
into the paving, into the house's foundations undermining
both the night's light and dark side.

You strike one, the pickaxe
discloses a sweet flesh. The shoot
breathes out like a slumbering
calf: so

they abide.

That day the air looked like wisps of hay that had fallen
    from a wagon.
It was hay, the kind used to line gift boxes. From the corner
    of the street the sounds
of normal life called, that is, the scream of children, the
    harangues of the married,
yelling of saleswomen. And there was something else,
    something
which I can't remember now.

Come to think of it, maybe it was the words or their
    portraits.
Yes, portraits of words that I preferred to hear. There they
    were, floating
above the bleat of dailiness: turned the other way round,
    walking the other way round,
portraits of words emerging from a camera obscura.
    Normally they wouldn't be captured,
but that day the wisps of hay, falling from the wagon,
    looked like summer air.

That day was a little bit odd. After walking down the street
    I stopped in a movement,
at one particular moment of getting older.
And I sensed it (the moment of getting older) like a scientist
    over a microscope:

the precise, split-second border between the former and the
    future me.
In that borderline, tangible second, I was nothing; only an echo
of a former self and the germ of the future, the old me.

It lasted for only that one moment. Then the air rustled like
    golden hay
and into the street a horse came. Klip-klop, klip-klop, with a
    face like a lovely icon;
he looked at me and put my life back in order: I heard again
the sounds of normal life, the scream of children, the harangues
    of saleswomen, yelling
of the married—and over all of that, in the hay-like air, still
    something else, still
something more.

FISH MARKET

Even before the sun rises,
in this strange, almost non-existent
hour, two different worlds
meet here: of people
and of fish. Those who've caught twist
and turn in a trance: their bodies shimmer
as if covered with scales, with croaking voices
they declare their wealth—delicious, weighty
flesh, glistening blood. They play pat-a-cake
on the fresh seafood pulp,
zestful and rosy-fingered
pleasures of the morning. The first handful of sun
falls on their laughing,
screeching faces, on muscular arms
in sticky shirts, rapaciously
hurling themselves into the everyday
life-giving battle.
The smell of fish intoxicates your senses.
In a moment you lose a continental distance:
the early morning mounts to your head,
a radiance of flesh; the salesmen's eyes,
slanted and dark, promising more.
You feel like stopping, giving in
to pleasure, to the sweaty
arms of the youngest of them,

drinking wine, shouting with them, dancing
on a slippery table;
as if in a dream cheerfully toasting
the wet souls of dead fish.

On Tuesday they go out to the market, leaving
their homes with shining eyes, women with coloured
turbans, with cats on their shoulders, pieces of
malachite hanging in their ears, going to pick out
fish and buckwheat, the rustle of paper bags
luring them like wasps to juicy pulp. They prod
fabrics, bulbous turnips and chard leaves, they keep
weighing handfuls of berries and grain, in the delicious sunshine
their hair glowing, wonder-working women, during the day
transforming like phantasmagoric beings:
for a moment spring or summer, silk or cotton.
They live in the present, they spread their arms towards the sun
as in a tantric dance, they talk and sing,
their heads decorated with baskets of fruit, they check
the feathers of proffered hens, they peer into prams
and they mutter their secrets as a delirious mantra.

At home afterwards
they unpack their booty from the hemp baskets,
spreading them on the table, caressing the bellies of the fish; by
    evening
beautiful women supple, moist, one day older and wiser,
making a fire to welcome the man who comes
tired and alone to drink from their alluring pitcher,

drinking it down and losing himself in a sleep, full of
    antlered beasts,
snared snipe and traps set. The lightning-flash women
then comb their hair before the mirror
and in a Bacchic prayer praise Tuesday.

ASO

Here under the volcano the earth breathes hard,
little by little emitting an inaudible,
firespring secret at the mercy
of those who've cut a piece out of it, making their homes
on its carotid artery, building
unabashed dwellings, houses of cards.
But the treasure of the volcano, traces of deep gold, velvet
and glass, doesn't sleep, looking a god
in the face with a yellow eye, sometimes
winking. Volcano; people
love it, they carry their sorrows
in translucent pitchers up to the crater,
they pray
to the gods of fire. White smoke rises to the clouds
and mingles with them as if there weren't
the difference between hell and heaven, only
the hellish gate
is closer. Whoever enters becomes
headless. Listening to the gurgle of the earth underfoot,
liquid, supple like mead spilt
in the secret bowels of the earth,
I think, the ash, the ash
doesn't scare them, on the alluring breasts
of the benign volcano as they cultivate their clairvoyant rice,
the volcano hugging them the way a moody mother

loves and punishes her little
mousy babies; so I think.

They aren't afraid of fire, they have
so much more.

CRAB SOUP

In a small windowless bar,
is it me who seeks
a pearl in every seashell?

It's snowing outside; safe,
anonymous streets. But inside
a bizarre mixture of ornaments.
The lord of the bar, father of the tavern,
ruler of this filthy kingdom,
is an old man recalling
all the twists and turns of history.
All you have to do is be here, enjoy
the vernacular—he'll tell everything,
will show his scars. His wife
a tiny elderly fairy
in her hand a loach and knife.
She chuckles quietly, on her face
a pale geisha mask,
indestructible, hiding
a sparkling blinking.

In a few years, like everyone else,
these two will find
their definitive
black shoes.

But now they are here, their fragile circumstances
have prepared for us
a performance called, This Evening.
It smokes and fizzes, sweet on the palate
like their crab soup,

in each shell a full moon.

DARKNESS

Only now is the real loneliness
when my tanned legs without clothes say:
we want to rest;
but there's is no bed, my loves, I answer them

like dogs who don't understand that home
is a chimera, that home
is not, that home
is just a thought
a chipping,
a small, flammable piece of wood thrown from the saw
as waste.

Such luck, in not understanding what
home is. I envy my beautiful legs
and dogs.

This sweet blindness of embryos.

LANDSCAPE IN WHITE

Now I can say everything
about snow, about this plain.
The banging on the glass has stopped,
the bottle is broken, without fear
its life is ended. Those full lungs,
the miracle of oxygen!

I look back a couple more times,
the station, plaintive crows.
The milk-toothed land submerges in fog,
down the slope roll
frozen mirrors, transparent
fingernails of waters.

Now I can speak;
a patch of bare earth
yawns
far from here,

inkwell, eye pupil,
staring
at my nights,
bitter rains,
a barren, unpeopled memory.

THE RUIN

I've been living in the ruin for three months now,
in a dilapidated house. It stands so close to the track
that with every train I wait
for the world to collapse. I live on the throat
of a time bomb. Every day I breathe
layers of dust that are born here with unrelenting precision
again and again, eternal as a spider.
Frogs and mice rustle in the cellar,
on the walls of the room where I sleep
geckos, centipedes and lizards hang like ribbons.
I don't feel alone here. The walls breathe in my sleep
healing words; the house
likes me being here.

It isn't sad. The heap of clay that serves
as a bathroom, looks friendly. It protects
from the heat, the nosy,
old injustices that I have torn from myself
like tiresome wingcases.

Under them moist,
slightly wrinkled wings have remained,
veined and tender, in a soft swoon.
I live here half in a trance, spreading them
with a light heart.

Every day
the ruin awaits me; my first
sweet home apart from the smell it gives off
and an uncertain scent that knows of me.

RETURN TO THE ISLANDS

While I'm sleeping, my night mind
leaves me, walks away
around the pond, around the greenish
nests of frogs, approaches them, asks
each of them, how
their little lives are in the shallows. This country
is not foreign for me. The moon, huge
as an airship, hangs by a thread.
Under its white balloon, as ever,
a smiling bunny.

In the morning I awake when a robin
slips into my bedroom, balancing
on outspread wings. I feel pain

as from a wound: as when in beauty
something is still missing.

MERCY

Gently a rose touches a pear, both
so close to the source of heat, but neither is
stove nor radiator. November is just behind the window,
this crumpled banknote, this
lady's slipper; when you hurl china to the ground,
it'll flash dramatically like the face of a capricious woman,
who went to a ball one last time. The last
is always the most beautiful; but you'd hardly ever know it.

Behind the window
the dead adjust their crumpled collars, shake off themselves
dried crumbs of a pagan feast, for which
they didn't ask; they'll take it easy again for a year. He who limps
walks down the darkening street and all at once feels
happy for no reason at all.

Eva Lukáčová was born in 1965 in Trnava in Slovakia. She studied English and Japanese at Comenius University in Bratislava and later Japanese language and literature at Hokkaido University and Osaka University, gaining her doctorate there in 2002 with a thesis written in Japanese. Her career in poetry began in the 1980s with selections in anthologies of young Slovak literature published under her given name, Eva Lukáčová, under which she also published her first collection *Divosestra* (Wildsister, 1999). Unlike many of her contemporaries, Eva's debut came relatively late, with her swerving around the mild attempts to *épater la bourgeoisie* by the largely male 'Barbarian' generation of Slovak poets. She pre-empted the emergence of a much stronger wave of women poets in the first decade of this century, the 'ANesthetic' generation, who later made their reputations.

Divosestra was hailed, with one critic quoting from a poem whose title became the title of her second book, 'The Deviltree': 'Who knows if this amazing tree really sprouted under her feet by morning, but we had to wait six years for its book form. Still, the wait was worth it.' *Divosestra* won a number of prestigious literary prizes including the Ivan Krasko Prize and the Maša Haľamová Prize.

Her second collection, *Diabloň* (Deviltree), was published in 2005 under her nom de plume, Eva Luka, which she has since used for all her subsequent works. This was followed by *Havranjel* (Ravenangel) in 2011 and a novel for children, *Pani Kurčaťová* (Mrs Chicken), in 2018. She published her fourth poetry collection, *Jazver* (I-Beast), in 2019 and her first book of poems for children, *Jemňacinky / Brutálničky* (Tender / Brutal Little Ones), illustrated by herself, in 2021. Her most recent book is a translation from Japanese into Slovak of Takashi Hiraide's *The Guest Cat*. Luke's work often features her own illustrations, with her striking visual style particularly evident in *I-Beast* and her children's poetry collections.

Eva Lukačová may well be one of the last great European poets of resistance: that is, a resistance to conform artistically and a resilience against the potential psychological pressures resulting from the circumstances of her life and times. Eva's resistance to being categorized within a specific poetic movement—particularly those heavily associated with a single gender—reflects the individual nature of her work, and this artistic independence even challenges gender identity in the personae that inhabit her poems. In her third collection, she included 'Wildbrother', a companion poem to 'Wildsister', where she pushes at the limits of a purely male consciousness, as opposed to a female consciousness, imagining a male doppelganger for herself. Identity becomes a transgressive potential: 'It smells like everyone / that I could be if / once I'd been born as him,' which is both taboo—'ravenangelic incest'—and a source of regret.

Eva's poems, crafted in this crucible, both channel and summon positive and dark energies in images of great power. The human and non-human natural worlds are fused in her poems, even at a linguistic level, as seen in the punning neologisms of her volumes' titles. In her debut collection, *Divosestra* (Wildsister), the fusion of 'wild' and 'sister' for the title poem and three companion poems seems innocuous, almost feebly fashionable. However, with 'Diabloň' (Deviltree), the fusion of 'devil' and 'jabloň' (apple tree) introduces a more inventive merging. *Diabloň* became the title of her second collection, and this in turn led to one of its poems, 'Havranjel' (Ravenangel), becoming the title poem of her third, and one of that collection's poems, 'Jazver' (I-Beast), becoming the title of her fourth. This is not simply a case of poetic caprice—they signify a continuity of theme and imagery throughout her work. This is a risky strategy, not least at the lexical level. 'Jazver' is a blend of 'Ja' and 'zver,' but also resonates with 'jazva' (scar) and 'jazvec' (badger), creating layers of meaning.

In Luka's poems, animals and angels become recurring motifs. Her imaginative thread often evokes Rilke, in whose work angels are a source of terror and darkness:

Every angel is terrible.
And thus I behave and gulp down the call
of dark sobs.

But whereas Rilke strains upwards out of his anguish, Luka plunges deep into the physical world: Rilke's imagination is metaphysical, Luka's is pantheistic and protoplasmic. A central figure in her second and third collections is the Ravenangel, an image that recalls the great Slovak poet Ivan Laučík's cave of origins, Havránok. The fusion of a bird of ill-omen and angel might evoke Poe's unwitting doomsayer or the jeering protagonist of Ted Hughes's 'Crow', which has been translated into Slovak. Indeed, Luka often employs motifs of blackness and darkness to delineate negative feeling, but she does so because her poems often occupy the space 'between the feverish night and the healing morning.'

It may be useful to compare Luka's work with that of Sharon Olds. Beyond a similar sexual explicitness, Luka, like Olds, crafts poems that relentlessly progress towards an emotionally logical conclusion, not to mention an occasional bitter end. The poet and critic Ján Gavura has remarked on the dreamlike yet highly organized quality of her mature work, and the academic Eva Urbanová has identified the continuing presence of 'wildsisters' in her oeuvre: examples in this selection include 'Virginia', 'Circe' and 'The Minotaur's Daughter'. Urbanová has also pointed out the symbolic significance of water in Eva's poetry, the classical element from which life emerges, identified with the amniotic fluid of the womb, but also with forgetfulness and death.

In the opening poem of this selection, 'The Water Anomaly', the protagonist is born as a fish, but the element is 'disgusting, murky', and she must swim away to be 'something of a snake, a scaly woman'. Later in this selection, 'Virginia' alludes to the suicide of Virginia Woolf, detailing the act of filling her dress pockets with stones in preparation for drowning. However, the narrative shifts to a first-person perspective of drowning—'A watery eye regards me'—culminating in a transformation: 'some aquatic animal wings' allow her to 'once more rise up, once more / to float', with the conclusion, 'And suicide is just a superstition'.

Luka's first collection, *Wildsister*, includes many poems written during her studies in Japan and have much in common with other travel poetry, with its focus on cultural contrasts. Yet, in a poem such as 'Fish Market', the exoticism of the locale is subsumed by the visceral conjunction 'of people / and of fish'—seafood flesh and the fish-sellers' muscular bodies. This preoccupation with physicality becomes an abiding strand in her later poetry. In 'Ikitsuki Island', the protagonist is 'reached at from a window— / all at once I've got a hand in another house', introducing the seedling of another strand in her work, that of fusing with otherness. Rimbaud's dictum *Je est un autre* underpins much of Luka's poetry. The pivotal poem 'The Deviltree', a fantasy occasioned by the jealous observation of two lovers, anticipates the themes of her later work: water, extravagant forms of life and obsessive behaviour that ultimately 'sprout / the deviltree'.

In reviewing her second collection, the critic Jaroslav Šrank seemed nonplussed by her authorial change of name, where she dropped the final two syllables of her surname—with 'Luka' suggesting 'luk' (an archer's bow). Šrank stubbornly referred to her throughout by her original surname, unlike Gavura or Urbanová. Without belabouring Šrank on his unreconstructed male habits, the change of name placed Luka beyond the orthodox register of Slovak woman poets, thus permitting herself to explore themes of mutability, such as merging with animals and interrogating gender fluidity.

The poems in *Deviltree* show a marked development in technique and ambition: 'Bamboos' harks back to her sojourn in Japan, yet 'they shoot, irresistible / as a snake', while 'Centaur' is a small masterpiece of sexual desire with its attendant fear of psychic pain— 'from my palm he carefully / bites out a pearl'. *Ravenangel* and *I-Beast* intensify the fusion of human and animal life with the terrifying I-Beast coming to find 'only / tatters of my night, my body, my hands'. The protagonist is unable to hear what it says except that 'it is about love; but / could be // likewise about killing'.

Luka's third collection, *Ravenangel*, appeared after an appalling personal tragedy, which might have silenced a less resilient poet. Mention is made of it in the dedicatory note to the collection, but, apart from one or two poems, Eva's progress as a poet doesn't seem to have been severely disrupted. She prefers critics of her work not to dwell on the tragedy. From *Ravenangel*, two poems have been translated which engage with feminist concerns. 'Mechanical Doll' is almost Plathian in its first seven lines, but then there is a palpable drawing of breath halfway through the seventh line with, 'Unfortunately . . . ' and then a switch to a dispassionate—almost academic—register, before her assertion that she can't be other than herself: 'I also wanted to be / for you what I couldn't', followed by a savage coda. The poem which follows in this selection, 'Man and Woman', is a curious departure from her predominant style in being almost without imagery. Instead, there is a series of assertions about male and female identity, concluding with the riddle, 'Because I'm a woman, I've got no choice but to wait; / or leave as well. The second / is harder'.

Eight years passed before Luka published her fourth collection, *Jazver*. Familiar motifs reappear, with many poems unfolding as phantasmagoric narratives. The fish market of the first collection has been relocated to somewhere more local and more magical as in 'Tuesday', where the women are domestic yet full of power and wild impulse: 'The lightning-women / then comb their hair before the mirror / and in a Bacchic prayer praise Tuesday'. Eva's line has lengthened in many of the poems in this collection and have the quality of disturbing vignettes as in 'Necromancer'. A number of the poems are ekphrastic, departing in particular from paintings by Leonora Carrington, whose first partner was the Surrealist painter, Max Ernst, and whose paintings have been rediscovered this century so that her reputation as a painter now eclipses that of Ernst. Poems in this translation written after Carrington's paintings include, 'Portrait of the Late Mrs Partridge', 'Necromancer', 'And Then They Saw the Minotaur's Daughter', 'Bird Bath', 'My Step-Sister's Hen' and 'Tuesday'.

Urbanová has speculated on the title of the next collection and suggested that it could well be 'Necromantik' (necromancer), a title that Eva Luka has recently confirmed to her translator. The poems intended at present for *Necromantik* in this selection seem to continue the short story quality as in the sequences 'Caldarium', 'Tepidarium', 'Frigidarium' and the 'Mrs Partridge' quintet.

Eva Luka is one of the most original poets writing in Europe today and could well become a powerful force for younger poets.

My translations owe much to the attention given to them by my daughter, Katarína Šoltis Smith, and to the poet herself, both of whom have pointed out my usual plethora of translation howlers and interrogated my decisions in order to improve the quality of the translations before you.

Thanks are due for financial support from the Slovak Literary Centre (Slovenské literárne centrum), Fond LITA and the TROJICA residency programme in Banská Štiavnica for a month's stay in the Rubigall klub between February and March 2024 in order to complete the book.